MW00534816

THE
INFANT
SCHOLAR

THE INFANT SCHOLAR

Poems

KATHY NILSSON

Michael you DOLL you a groom for a penthouse! Kathy too

TP

TUPELO PRESS
NORTH ADAMS, MASSACHUSETTS

The Infant Scholar.
Copyright © 2015 Kathy Nilsson. All rights reserved.

Nilsson, Kathy, 1951-
 [Poems. Selections]
 The infant scholar : poems / Kathy Nilsson. —First paperback edition.
    pages cm — (Berkshire Prize, Honorable Mention: Tupelo Press Award for
First or Second Book)
Summary: "Poems crafted to convey the uncanny associative abilities that result from
synesthesia. An homage to those born brilliant and vulnerable, who have a great
comprehension at odds with their young age" — Provided by publisher.
 ISBN 978-1-936797-54-7 (pbk. : alk. paper)
 1. Synesthesia — Poetry. I. Title.
 PS3614.I572A6 2015
 811'.6 — dc23
        2014044194

Cover and text designed and composed in Subway Novella and Adobe Garamond
    Premier Pro by Howard Klein.
Cover photograph used with permission of the poet.

First paperback edition: January 2015.

Other than brief excerpts for reviews and commentaries, no part of this book may be
reproduced by any means without permission of the publisher. Please address requests for
reprint permission or for course-adoption discounts to:

Tupelo Press
P.O. Box 1767, North Adams, Massachusetts 01247
Telephone: (413) 664–9611 / editor@tupelopress.org / www.tupelopress.org

Tupelo Press is an award-winning independent literary press that publishes fine fiction,
nonfiction, and poetry in books that are a joy to hold as well as read. Tupelo Press is a
registered 501(c)(3) nonprofit organization, and we rely on public support to carry out
our mission of publishing extraordinary work that may be outside the realm of the large
commercial publishers. Financial donations are welcome and are tax deductible.

for Claes and John

CONTENTS

Having Lived Very Long

2   STILL LIFE—
3   WHERE ARE
4   SEEING BIRDS
5   LITTLE ICE AGE—
6   I AM AVAILABLE
7   YOU CAN HIDE
8   THE FIRST TIME

Last Ride Together

10   THUS
11   WITH EXTROVERSION
12   IN THE BEGINNING
13   WHO HAS READ
14   THE PILLS
15   WHEN I LIVED WITH YOU
16   EVERYTHING WAS
17   POSTCARDS
18   MOTHER WITH DEMENTIA

Some at Rest

20   WHEN THE LAST AUTUMN
21   THE LATE SUN
22   SURGERY
23   LIVING MANY
24   THE MAN GATHERS
25   WINDOW-SHOPPING
26   THE PROGRESSION
27   IT TOOK A LONG TIME—
28   BORROWED SCENERY

Parliament of All Things

30   IF SMALL MEN
31   I WENT TO THE DESERT
32   BLACK LEMONS—
34   APPOINTED

35 HORSE, HIROSHIMA—
36 ALL THE HAPPINESS OF ARABIA—
37 WATERSIDE LIVING—
38 YOU FISH YOU FISH—
39 DRAWN TO AN ISLAND

A Whim of the Emperor

42 THE WORLD
43 BORN EARLY
44 WITH EYES CLOSED
45 EACH DAY BEGINS
46 THE PROFESSORS OF NATURE
47 I EXPECTED
48 I HEAR

Coupling Like Snowflakes

50 WHEN YOU GO OUTSIDE
51 DON'T TOUCH
52 LITTLE SURVIVES—
53 I AM
54 A NIGHT
55 I KNOW
56 RETURNING

Here to Japan

58 SEPTEMBER
59 NIGHT FALLS
60 AFTER HIS FEAT
61 THE DAY
62 WOMEN
63 SOCIETY FINCHES—
64 MAYBE I AM
65 I SLEEP

68 Acknowledgments

Having Lived Very Long

STILL LIFE—

I'm having trouble looking animals in the eye.

Their empty suits in outer space!

Monkeys injected with a virus to show off

Our eminent domain, the nervous system.

Teacup pigs we breed and obsessive mice

Worrying themselves bald in a miniature opera.

For pleasures of the tongue we are

Winking cattle out of meadows

Slashing their throats and swiftly quartering them.

In riding habits with gold flame pins we ride horses

To hounds, chase a fennec fox until his red

Coat flares up against the extinction

Of light. Once in a circus we made

An elephant disappear and he did not mind.

WHERE ARE the elephants

Slipping tusks underneath one another

Breaking off ivory

And perfect little replicas of the elephants

Allowing themselves to be led

To a circus

Devout on their knees—

To my husband and son

I was allmothers

with a huge seat of memory.

SEEING BIRDS flush you fall to your knees

You couldn't eat a hazel grouse for what

You make of it— the soft birth of your own great

Reliable outcome— configured yourself

Out of the quiet blood of beasts, you could

Be conducted on a little cord held by a child—

Suddenly, you have the mildness of a giraffe

With its discreet, unrequited interest in other animals.

LITTLE ICE AGE—

I have one good memory— a total

Eclipse of the sun— when out of brilliance

Dusk came swiftly and on the whole

At seven years it felt good on a summer afternoon

To be outrun by a horse from another century—

The next morning I washed up

On land like a pod of seals

Struck with a longing for dark at noon—

If the cessation of feeling is temporary

It resembles sleep— if permanent, it resembles

A little ice age— and the end of some

Crewelwork by a mother who put honey

Into my hands so the bees would love me.

I AM AVAILABLE to the public like Houdini

You can't imagine the trouble it takes to make a little breeze

Wardrobes aren't built in a day

My appearance passes radar like orphan frogs living behind swollen books in
    New Orleans

My arm is a sinker fishing for my slipper

I have the skin of an ocean

I grow cold and lethargic like a lobster

Free from attachment I live as though I were already dead

Is this a visit or an epidemic?

My identity is tagged on the nether side of a floating nightclub

Copyright is for losers

I welcome friendly hallucinations of an erotic nature

I fill the catalog of human expressions

I scare a lizard.

YOU CAN HIDE when a man with mallows

Offers to help you on a horizontal journey

Into the barn where you came from—

Enter the maze of hornbeam

Planted for William of Orange—

The smaller you are, the more

Familiar with strangers, the easier

It is to buffalo you with information—

A boy in school carried his stool around

Wrapped in silver paper inside a pencil box

Just in case he would say—

The more blue sky deserves a translation.

THE FIRST TIME the infant scholar

Touches ground he's in danger

Chimps get inside his fits of mirth

He floats in water on inflated animals

Weeping hormones like golden hamsters

His little armpits spice boxes!

What will people say to him

Steering around a crowded room

Growing more lifelike, more human—

When afraid he attempts to hide

By rolling up in floor rugs

And sometimes protruding from

The soft mound with perfumed

Coatings of tiny looted pharaohs

He leaves us like a young autumn

Octopus without having lived very long.

Last Ride Together

THUS I have inside me

Giraffes shyly taking water—

If I move, it can only be

Because they move—

If they move, it must be

The little giraffe living

Inside them that moves them.

WITH EXTROVERSION found in herring

Face recognition among

Sheep— dreams of mice asleep in cabins

And laughter in rats after a fall—

Face-up like a head of lettuce in the garden

A woman combs her hair of heavenly phenomena

At the edge of the cosmos and stars in a way

Becoming.

IN THE BEGINNING it was like being

Alive— any moment something fine was

To come to me— history with its infantry

Recollection of blue bending over me

From which good would issue—

I longed to be versatile— married late

Tried to welcome all the children that would

Come begging to be chloroformed

Like a kitten but you were the only one—

As winters moved across a luminous empty

Viewing gallery, in spring emeralds

Living underground stimulated by radiation

Sprang up as panic grass a shade of green

That would break young horses, I saw how

The archeologists would arrive to find fibers

Of my robe thrilling and head on the ground

With late apples, a color of the universe at large.

WHO HAS READ a suicide note

He would want to have written

Or poured gasoline inside a small

Car sprinkling it over himself

To a great extent, something of

The city, fair weather

Egging him on to turn on

The master like a puppet

Dispatch him with a match lit

Like the blaze on a colt's forehead

Or Leonid of a shooting star.

THE PILLS you take to help you sleep, sleep for you

When daylight eases in illuminating planks

Your kids will walk into the ocean, walls made

With tortured wood and yards force-fed like geese

Ballooning with fat, a mammoth in the driveway

Laced with insects and glistening *THANK-YOU*

RED— by afternoon the thief has fled with sacks

Of diamonds the size of birds' eggs— your life is

Fake instead of a masterpiece and your dog is a sphinx.

WHEN I LIVED WITH YOU we kept

The schnapps cold and on the move

Like albino deer in Wisconsin—

Made salads from shy young weeds

Sliced our hearts of lamb thin—

Considering what kills the least

Number with the most ease.

EVERYTHING WAS fresh

When we took it— Rain rinsed

And dried as if with saddle soap

And vodka giving the landscape

A sleepy appearance on which

Hunters feed— flight was possible

Before we closed the distance

Between animals and people—

An elephant returning to the spot

To turn and feel a mother's skull

Using her trunk like a tongue— and

The big cat with a stove of hair.

POSTCARDS from the Grand Canyon mimic happiness

With a touch of overkill— no apology for solving any mystery

Downgrading the future with dashes across countryside

To shoot serene landscapes— with cries coming from

Animals comprehending being wild— though we find them

Unfit for exhibit with other bears, monkeys, flamingoes

          Dead but alive with hallucinatory clarity.

MOTHER WITH DEMENTIA wrote a note

Saying goodbye to herself— *Bye bye, Pauline,*

We'll see you later— and left it by her chair

A few days before the fatal rupture that led

To the silence of a young boy in Bangladesh and his pet

Goat underway on their last ride together.

Some at Rest

WHEN THE LAST AUTUMN flies

Strike the window looking for sugar

I will be outside clinging like an ungulate

To the back of a woman heading home

In plimsoles after a long Monday

Though she keeps all the lights on

As a small consolation to come home

To and scattered rain lands like the pile

On budding antlers of hinds under

Sky the egg colors of pheasants.

THE LATE SUN gave out

At the end of a highway

Under a great director

Shocking and giving spice

To everything— like a note

Filed in a coroner's office—

Dear Betty, I hate you, love,

George— from someone

In a matched pair (said of

Horses by country people)

Who slid into the Pacific

Like a girl in a claw-footed

Bathtub blowing dry her hair.

SURGERY as

As dusting of snow
Fastened to roofs

On a row of Delft houses

Ash from mantles
Insects that fly

Only once

And bite off their wings
When they land

The mind lies down
                    Old fish

The heart is
On the table

Aloft, in a red lake.

LIVING MANY months

Under snow

A penitentiary when

Squirrels blab like men

Confessing to one

Another— I rise from bed

Gowned in slubbed

Satin like tinder

Flung into water.

THE MAN GATHERS flowers strewn by a storm

Out of injury comes the peaceful care of a wound

His smooth brown heart rests like a ship at the bottom

Of the ocean— he looks as if about to set sail—

Apples cast blue ovals on the table—fastidious

And uneventful, the sound of a bell is a natural

Partition in a moment of disappearing— is there

A chance of a beautiful prognosis— what kind of

Behavior is sleep when someone perceives he must,

Having sung all his life, desist, and then shrinking

Uniformly become common salt, earth, carbon, nil?

WINDOW-SHOPPING, a man feigns interest gazing into a haberdashery

To disguise the extent of his chest pain— he must avoid flowers, debris,

Potato skins, cat litter, and even a granddaughter's tears to ward off rejection

Of a suitable heart— daylight looks pale to him— his reflection is a watering place

On old maps when it took quite a while for the sea to become blue and blue

To become cold— he will give under weight of a few snowflakes, his shoulders

Lifted like a pair of falcons, his overcoat reverting to the shape of the animal

From which it came.

THE PROGRESSION I watch

Like flames in a fireplace

The dumb world outside

Is an embarrassment of

Kindly maples under which

An earthling throws it away

With a flagrant *what if*—

Phobias affect the weather

Some countries are gone

Like the possibilities of being

Beautiful and young—

Our only son is unleashed

In slow traffic along a woman

Searchlights not stars

Are glancing the window

Every place is discovered

Everything is made in China

Everyone looks familiar.

IT TOOK A LONG TIME— earth

Was a nervous giant— we didn't

Know her limits— a doe

Covered in doeskin, the back

Of a great baleen whale—

Rowboats hung up there with

Eerie lightness— rice, glitter, bone

Thrown in— wood breaking up

Like a teacup in the shipwreck

Of a book—it only takes a minute

And then you are a nudist, negatively

Buoyant, holding your breath

In a violent pastime at your

Failure depth sinking to where

No one swims, losing conscious-

Ness during hush-hush meetings

Believe you me— coming to

In an alpine meadow.

BORROWED SCENERY at night

Treading across the Persian rugs

A murderer living on the smell of

An apple before sleep keeps her

From wandering in the dark, a ghost

Free of bones and handfuls of hair

Shadows made by nothing— when

Birds fly up, they disappear

With no will to be great—like pairs

Of clouded tigers seen through

A finder— many moving in their

Last moments but some at rest.

Parliament of All Things

IF SMALL MEN wearing nothing emerge from a jungle asking

Shall we wrap your penises? Then go without any argument

Of hydraulics, pneumatics or English telescopes, the lost art

Of caterpillar inflation for mounting on cork in a genitalia cabinet

Like fish susceptible to dazzle and with a complete memory

Of the world's history at heights to which plants lift water— withdraw

Saying *I've given enough— Goodbye.*

I WENT TO THE DESERT to see

A flower open after a drop of rain

And to regard the mujahedeen softly

Whipping my bare ankles— where

Fossil water once fell as rain

For the Queen of Sheba and fed seed

Pearls sold door to door by divers

Near lambs roasted on spits

And bees flown on strings by young

Boys expressing their boredom

In colloquial Arabic which is said

To derive from the gestures

                    Of a drowning man.

BLACK LEMONS— in the desert

Sun is a bludgeon— I emerge

To the small knucklebones

In cotton, the luff of gowns

A confection of dark men

Leaning on a rail

The disproportion between me

And the space I inhabit

Has divine repetition

There is life

My date of birth is a shower after which

An orchid is found in the reed—

Oleander, cassia, black lemons

Are not meant to last

They are drawers of gold

My bed carved from thick trunks

A rosewood cathedral

Glows like shrimp in the sun

My milk carries a trace of the local

Grazing— it is salty

And foams in a bowl.

... APPOINTED for visits with an elder tantric yogi

Two girls from California in ivory wool lob

A shuttlecock beside the Snuggery— I am

Twenty-one and on my own with a diffuse

Inner life— when the clouds lift revealing

Mount Everest— I try to love necessity

Years later, under nine million cold stars

When two people are left on the summit

Alone to die, I will take it like an animal—

But tonight, I am arrested by the diamond

On a scrupulous brown hand and a clamor

Of bells as his Holiness, protégées and

Chaperone dip spoons in their waterglasses—

1978, Hotel Windamere, Darjeeling.

HORSE, HIROSHIMA— ran in circles

Mimicking the sky— groans from survivors

Asking forgiveness— on a summer day

Someone looking for love with a wheelbarrow!

Over-stimulated with radiation on a scale

Affecting the afterlife of the unborn—

This map shows the onset of recognition

Because trains are so long now, the world

Has become feminine— young boys lie down

On trestles to wait for them— over a hill

Winter will come down to ponds carrying

Their effects— few, light and breakable.

ALL THE HAPPINESS OF ARABIA—

A drop of water falls on a tuft of grass

Shivers like a starfish in The Empty Quarter

Stands like an elephant after death

The rising sun is astronomical

A swimming bell turning bright red

Showing the flashy contents of ingested prey—

I blow over the surface in a teacup and make sea.

WATERSIDE LIVING— in a heart-shaped

Candy-box interior of timber mansions on the Bosporus

Finished in looking-glasses fritted from an alp's pebbles

Glimpses of the stranger you were before you were born

You row a dinghy with catch-words spoken at length

To one in a coma hypnotic as the water— the organs

Of your shadow falling violet as snow on a chair.

YOU FISH YOU FISH— all you

Want is a decent life

And a lively death—

From the sidelines

We track you offshore

Filtering out glare with glasses

Like emeralds

Through which Nero

Watched the gladiators.

DRAWN TO AN ISLAND off Maine

Where everything is shrinking

Like ponies in the Shetlands

I live inside a snow globe

On the tip of an alp in the ocean

A panoramic view in little

The color of a soap bubble

A sapphire to the mainland

The edge lies in hieroglyphic

Crosses marking the ledge of a picnic

Where a comber swept Jackie out

To sea with Edward trying to save her—

I shuttle between day and night headed for

Parliament of all things.

A Whim of the Emperor

THE WORLD was transparent

Tobacco grew wild

A chime carried distinction

Somewhere coupled earthworms

A young lobster locked

In another version

Turning over a sea floor.

BORN EARLY we lie around

Dividing in and out with a mouth

Becoming a little women and

A little men— defrauding objects

Of a right not to move— riding

Chariots down a long access road

Panoramic— our surrounds— we

Begin walking like bold invalids

On a Swiss holiday— a two-headed

Snake exits both sleeves at one time.

WITH EYES CLOSED I came to life

Stirred by the feel of falling earth or snow

Ground and sky separated long ago

Hours sounded by bells— perhaps

This will be my golden hour

As a world full of water grazes me

With the keel of a petal—

        You can finish with me now.

EACH DAY BEGINS what should I do— tighter

Tighter— as parasol ants and weightlifters

Drag their food away— later I roast kid for dinner

With a desire really to look after chickens—

Instead I will enter the Olympics and ball up

In a nightgown— my friends will go into rapture

Apart from hair and a toenail I'll be found intact

On the last day of the races— being run out with

The ring-boned, stifled, blind, lame and halt.

THE PROFESSORS OF NATURE have

Given her license to carry the feather

Of a condor— her legs are the color

Of blond pine in a Danish ship— her

Chassis imitates the roses as children

Fling couch grass around her tinkling

In furbelows from the east and fanning

Herself in Brazil— she undulates across

The lawn baffling the air with her sapphire

Denying permission to these light angels.

I EXPECTED aging and sickness and death

But another summer breaks on the family

Reef with dire-horses, banshees, slinths

And sunsets enough to drive to despair

A man of this century— so I practice

On watermelons, scrape bone, suture cloth

Sear lamb and read clouds— they say

Push the arrows through continuing a path

Along the hair or pull back with a tug— to

Dislodge one load victim into a cart and

　　　　　Drag it down a bumpy road.

I HEAR it is peaceful in cemeteries

No feelings of taking it out on anyone

Everything we ever wanted to happen

Happening on the horizon— heaps

Of precious fur and shadows stitched

Carefully like the sail on a clipper ship—

Spring letting the first creatures as one

Might wear jewels on occasion— then

Being executed on a whim of the emperor.

Coupling Like Snowflakes

WHEN YOU GO OUTSIDE you must be credulous

You must believe in strange things

Look down— there are instances of great love

A heart is as large as an anthill in Switzerland

The pulse is a string of pearls

Conjugal visits by a radiant yellow man are bringing up your color

Primitive men say *we didn't do it and we don't know who did*

Change from evening to day is real

World the Greeks called *ornament* being pushed above the sea

People often found next to trees

Orient of morning

Statues are signing to you in dumb crambo from Rome

You must be tied with string to the house so you won't fly away.

DON'T TOUCH the mouse fur

It refers to recent life

Up to sixty-five million years ago

The fear and pain

An insect might feel

Being shoved into a crack

As vast as the Vale

Of Swat— and jonquils

Planted as decoys for goslings

Breaking ground in England.

LITTLE SURVIVES—

Monks' craniums sideling in the Alps

With nurse logs and frass and the white

Porcelain back of an English climber—

Those hauled into the Hide Room lined

With valuables of other mammals

Hanging by hooks like jackets—

One who to tried to lie down with a divine

Chemical host whose properties were

Apparent but hard to believe—

On day eighteen of weaning when she

Becomes tender and whimpers she

Appears to be in love with her doctor.

I AM beautiful for nothing

But the circulation of my blood

I can observe inside the membrane

Of a frog like a map in which streams

Are actually flowing in school—

I feel a kinship with a gorilla

Named Guy, a baby mammoth

Frozen just after birth and a butterfly

Which last sipped nectar with

Composure on the shore of an ancient

Lake, Florissant— my mind drowses

Like a kitten— on rainy nights

I watch for accidents like someone

In a hospital waiting for a heart.

A NIGHT drawn by horses

Nurses push the fluid in

Smarting under a vein

A string of near misses

Like little abortions—

My motto— *In God We Trust*

After I read it on a nickel—

Facts go forever picking up

Deformation on television

A few explosives thrown in—

    I'll be off now.

I KNOW I'm here

By the class of aves

Like flying fish—

Being drugged with

Attar and cinnamon—

Then wanked by

Bees and banged

By shadows—

Sometimes I behave

Normally like an oyster

On the half-shell

Or a pretty woman

With a light at her groin.

RETURNING to the marriage

A carbon woman and a carbon man

Listen to smithereens

Being discarded on the lawn

Like carcasses from a natural history

Museum imploring them to do something

Their thoughts carry on coupling

Like snowflakes.

Here to Japan

SEPTEMBER brings afternoon

In a chalice to the table

Rustling seeds of the camellia

And horse chestnut strung

In a rosary around the yard

Deflecting harm like diamonds

Sewn into a Romanov corset—

The owner of the skeleton in life

Never apprehends the day

From her infinite thermal surround

Overwintering in a brilliant

Carotene of early leaf drop

Limned by a dim tallow sun

And finds it merciful.

NIGHT FALLS like snow into the aftermath of fire

Automobiles catapult through time linking people

From lower animals come bells like racial slurs

Jewels are stuffed into bags on the horizon

This way to the egress— I exit sheathed only

In a light coat— under constellations the natural

World comforts me as a wire mother does a chimpanzee.

AFTER HIS FEAT performed on a high wire above the city

The aerialist has gone upstate to study the bending moment in wood

And build into his cabin walls little plinths for holding caviar

As if you could throw perfume on a violet! Today

There is no trace of spectators who saw him genuflecting there

Realizing any moment he could plummet like his sweater into the noble

Gases and the heads turned up like reserved cabbages.

THE DAY drained of color

And tens of thousands of years

Separate us from natural selection—

Tonight we'll sleep in a position

Retained from the old cloacal days

And go through the periodic table

Targeting us in our demographic

Wrapped in the universe.

WOMEN are horizontal

Drinking hairspray and Lysol

Their hearts shrink and slow

Blacking out isn't unpleasant

By winter they can tell

In the nerves of the face

Where a surface is by feel

The thickness of air above

And below an ordeal

As pigeons get their bearings

From an atlas in the sky—

Constellations are arranged

Like a diamond solitaire

Necklace lying around

In a void with Arabic names—

Aldebran, Deneb, Altair.

SOCIETY FINCHES—

Though we loved that rabbit we loved eating it too

Drinking at home we look up at the braces of heaven

Winter is staging a wedding of Jacobin pigeons

Our kidneys are little darlings shuttling us into day

We wake disappointed because we're still alive

On this side of *to be*— with a niggling of fatality

At home, the most common location followed by tall

Buildings and bodies of water, on Monday or Sunday

Or frozen in place on Mount Everest in May

And left there as if glued inside a snow globe

Those who want to die do not want to die— we

Imagine we have one week to live and start crying

After many years of talking with us the psychiatrist

Said he found us stranger than the birds in his garden.

MAYBE I AM like a monster

Too experienced— carrying

The smell of polecat and murder

Planning horrible things I would

Do if you asked me to

In two-way conversations

With God assuming both parts—

For three thousand years

We couldn't hear ourselves

For the sound of water birds

And now even in Siberia

It is quiet except for a clatter

Of insects, rasp of an engine.

I SLEEP like a woman

Stepping out of a wolf

In regions where feet

Would never, never

Have trod and in a small

Wilderness where I have

No purpose whatsoever

I wake with the weak

Assertions of a lobster

Going into live steam

Taking on a shade of flame

As the Lord of Bingo

Progresses through his realm

And glows like an orange

From here to Japan.

ACKNOWLEDGMENTS

Grateful acknowledgement is made to the editors of the journals in which these poems first appeared, in some cases in another form.

Boston Review and *Poetry Daily*: "Seeing Birds"

Center: "Living Many

Columbia: "The First Time" and "In the Beginning"

Gulf Coast: "The Man Gathers"

Meridian: "Waterside Living"

Poetry: "Little Ice Age" and "Still Life"

Post Road: "Black Lemons"

Ploughshares: "Thus"

Salamander: "Borrowed Scenery"

Volt: "With Eyes Closed"

Del Sol Reviews: "All the Happiness of Arabia"

Some of these poems appeared in *The Abattoir*, a chapbook published by Finishing Line Press (2008).

OTHER BOOKS FROM TUPELO PRESS

Fasting for Ramadan: Notes from a Spiritual Practice (memoir), Kazim Ali

Moonbook and Sunbook (poems), Willis Barnstone

Another English: Anglophone Poems from Around the World (anthology),
    edited by Catherine Barnett and Tiphanie Yanique

Circle's Apprentice (poems), Dan Beachy-Quick

The Vital System (poems), CM Burroughs

Stone Lyre: Poems wof René Char, translated by Nancy Naomi Carlson

Living Wages (poems), Michael Chitwood

New Cathay: Contemporary Chinese Poetry (anthology), edited by Ming Di

Gossip and Metaphysics: Russian Modernist Poems and Prose,
    edited by Katie Farris, Ilya Kaminsky, and Valzhyna Mort

Or, Gone (poems), Deborah Flanagan

The Posthumous Affair (novel), James Friel

Entwined: Three Lyric Sequences (poems), Carol Frost

Poverty Creek Journal (memoir), Thomas Gardner

Into Daylight (poems), Jeffrey Harrison

Ay (poems), Joan Houlihan

The Faulkes Chronicle (novel), David Huddle

Darktown Follies (poems), Amaud Jamaul Johnson

Dancing in Odessa (poems), Ilya Kaminsky

A God in the House: Poets Talk About Faith (interviews),
    edited by Ilya Kaminsky and Katherine Towler

domina Un/blued (poems), Ruth Ellen Kocher

Phyla of Joy (poems), Karen An-hwei Lee

Boat (poems), Christopher Merrill

Lucky Fish (poems), Aimee Nezhukumatathil

Ex-Voto (poems), Adélia Prado, translated by Ellen Doré Watson

Intimate: An American Family Photo Album (memoir), Paisley Rekdal

Thrill-Bent (novel), Jan Richman

Vivarium (poems), Natasha Sajé

Cream of Kohlrabi (stories), Floyd Skloot

The Perfect Life (essays), Peter Stitt

Soldier On (poems), Gale Marie Thompson

Swallowing the Sea (essays), Lee Upton

See our complete backlist at www.tupelopress.org

CPSIA information can be obtained
at www.ICGtesting.com
Printed in the USA
FFOW03n2007110315
11669FF

9 781936 797547